The Salvation of Genie

LEFT FOR DEAD BUT TOO YOUNG TO DIE

EUGENIA S. ROLLINS

Eugenia Rollins

Bridge To Life

Building Relationships in Different Geographical Environments

ISBN-10: 0-9976043-3-6
ISBN-13: 978-0-9976043-3-7

Second Edition

First printing by Lumen-Us Publications 2009

Published by:
Bridge-To-Life, Inc.
P.O. Box 1945
Muncie, IN 47308
www.bridge-to-life.net

Designed by: Kizmin M. Jones

Scriptures are taken from the King James Version of the Holy Bible unless otherwise noted.

Eugenia Rollins

Dedication

I dedicate this book to all those who have survived child abuse, it is my hope that you can glean from my story. It is my hope that you would become an advocate in your own way for children and others who have no voice.

May this book be a voice for all the men, women and children who have not shared their stories.

About the Author

Eugenia Rollins is a Gary, Indiana native-born resident. She attended and graduated from the Gary Community School Corporation. Eugenia attended Ball State University and Case Western Reserve University to obtain her Bachelors and Masters Degrees in Social Work.

As a young author, she has been writing for more than ten years. Eugenia enjoys writing poetry, letters to God, and other inspirational thoughts that she hopes would enhance the lives of others. Through her testimony of triumph, she desires to empower, enrich, and encourage the hearts of men, women, boys, and girls.

Acknowledgments

To my mother and father, Ms. Carol Rodgers and Mr. Cecil C. Rollins Jr., and extended family, thanks for all that you have done to help me be who I am today. I am grateful to God for your love and support always.

To my Godparents, Apostle S. M. Millben and Co-Pastor Denise Millben, I salute the both of you as wonderful spiritual and natural instructors. Thank you for all you have done for me. Words truly cannot express the love that I have for the both of you and your family. May God Bless your entire family for all that has been poured into me. (*P.S. I LOVE the Dump Cake!!!*)

To the Christ Temple Global Ministries family, I love and appreciate each and every one of you. I cannot type all of your names on paper, but your names have been printed in my heart forever. Thanks for all the food, fellowship, and fun times. Thanks for all the prayers, and thanks for allowing me to be me, blessings to each of you.

To Mrs. Mia V. Brooks, (my cousin), words cannot express my gratitude; all I can say is thank you!

To Ms. Kesha L. Reese, (my cousin), I love you like a sister. Thanks for being there for me. I will always appreciate the fun times that we have shared and look forward to many more.

To the pastors of the New Spirit Revival Center Church in Cleveland, Ohio Drs. Darrell and Belinda Scott and the New Spirit Church family, thank you for all that you have done for me during my graduate studies. I am so grateful that God saw fit to send me to New Spirit. I am a better person because of your ministry. I love all of you. Thanks for being pastors after God's heart. The both of you have a Godly vision and a voice that commands attention. Love Ya!!

Thanks to Minister Latre Mattis for all your prayers, smiles and songs of inspiration. Your ministry has blessed me more than words can ever express. Love You Always.

Last but not least, I would like to thank all the people that have mentored me through the years. I will not mention names, but you know who you are. However, I want to say thanks to the dynamic trio, the three of you have been a major blessing to me in recent days. Your prayers, Godly example, and mentorship have

Eugenia Rollins

changed my life. The three of you have made life in Cleveland, Ohio much easier. Sis. DeBorah Mosley, Elder LaRita Howard, Minister Florine Jones. Thanks!!!

Contents

Chapter One: Saved, but Mentally Ill............ page no. 14

Chapter Two: Innocence Interrupted............ page no. 20

Chapter Three: When the Bad

Outweighs the Good............................... page no. 26

Chapter Four: Help, Save Me from Myself! ..... page no. 42

Chapter Five: School Days/My Genesis.......... page no. 50

Chapter Six: Losing the Battle but

Winning the War................................. page no. 64

Chapter Seven: Beyond What I Could

Imagine.. page no. 79

Chapter Eight: In the Hallway: Between

the Promise and the Prize .... page no. 94

Chapter Nine: A Lesson Learned is a Lesson

Never to Repeat .... page no. 115

Eugenia Rollins

Introduction

It is better that a millstone be tied around your neck and you are buried in the sea, than if you hurt the least of the little ones!

Paraphrased from the Holy Scriptures

I was born on September 10, 1979. I came into this world a month premature and fighting for my life. It's ironic, but as I think about it, until recently, I have been battling for survival ever since.

Due to the fact that I was born too soon, my internal organs were underdeveloped causing me to suffer from numerous health problems including Failure to Thrive. For some undiscovered reason I was born cross-eyed. Also one of my major health issues involved my body not being able to digest food. On more than one occasion, this condition left me under-weight, malnourished, and at deaths door needing to be fed by IV (intravenously), to stay alive. As a matter of fact I spent most of my early years in and out of the hospital.

I remember one of my nurses, who I ran into a few years ago, recalled my childhood medical conditions and stated "We thought we were going to lose you many times, but you were a fighter." I believe that God put a strong will of survival in my spirit, because He had a purpose for my life. A purpose that I will began to share with you in the pages of this book.

The experiences that I will reveal are all true accounts, regardless of how unbelievable some of them may seem. Names have been changed to protect the innocent, and the not so innocent. As life has taught me, victims who are not healed and set free, often become the worst predators!

Eugenia Rollins

CHAPTER ONE

Saved, but Mentally Ill?

Dear Born-Again Believer, I have a question for you. Do you think a person can be "saved" and yet be mentally ill? Think about this, how many believers do you know that have been sick in the past, may be currently sick, or have been diagnosed with an illness or disease in their body?

Well, if a person can be sick in their body, how come in numerous cases we do not accept the fact that a person can be sick in their mind. And what may be even more controversial is the fact that, if God can provide medical knowledge and medicine to heal the body, can't He also provide medical knowledge and medicine to heal the mind? Is that really so bad?

Let me explain why this profound question is so important to me. Also, I guess the best place to start is right at the beginning.

I was raised in one of the low-income housing developments in Gary, Indiana. The project development that I lived in was filled with gangs, drugs, and all sorts of violence, the type of place where no young child should call their home. On a regular basis, my next-door neighbors were drunk and fought at all hours of the night. In addition, only a thin wall separated our apartments, therefore, we heard every profane word and argument that took place.

When I was approximately four-years-old I can recall having my first memory. I was sitting in a chair at the end of our long oddly shaped dining room table. I had on my red dress that tied up in the back. I think I remember that moment because a nationally known gospel-recording group called The Winans was singing on the radio, and I love that group to this day. At any rate, as I bobbed my head to the music, I recall my mother nude fixing and serving my big brother and me breakfast. As a matter of fact, she cooked and served every one of our meals nude, until we got older. I never thought much about it, because that was all I knew, so I thought it was normal.

Meals were very difficult, because my mother didn't know how to cook properly. The food tasted so bad that my older brother and I would sit at the dining room table talking and wishing we had a garbage disposal under one of the white tiles on the floor. Of course, our dream never came true, and we would have to endure the food. Ritually, I ate out of a small green bowl and my brother ate out of a medium sized yellow bowl, as my mother fed us the same foods every day. She never sat down to eat with us and typically the food was over-cooked or under-cooked. For instance, if she fixed canned corn and a watered down cup of Tang (an orange powdered drink mix), we would eat that for every meal until we ran out of it. If I protested that the corn tasted like water, her reply would be, "You betta be thankful, the kids in Africa would love to eat this" but somehow that never seemed to console me.

For some odd reason we were never allowed to enter into the kitchen or sit in the living room. We just ate all of our meals at that oddly shaped dining room table. One time when I was a bit older, I attempted to go in the kitchen just to see what it would feel like. As I went in, I can remember standing in front of the old brown cabinets under the dim lights trying to open the cabinets just to take a look inside. After all, that would have been a brand new experience for me. However, when she saw me, it was all over. My mother yelled at me so loudly, it could have shaken the entire block. She screamed so hard that spit flew out of her mouth. Finally the neighbors next to our apartment hit the wall as a sign for her to quiet down. In my small way I tried to stand up for myself by yelling back at her stating, "This is my house too and I want to see what we have to eat." That just made things worse, and she was angrier than ever. Needless to say, with that type of fury, she won and from that point on, I never attempted to go back in her kitchen. It was just not worth the fight!

Being forbidden to enter into major rooms in a place that was supposed to be my home made me feel like unwanted dirt that contaminated the room. It also made me question if my mother was hiding something from me, something that I was not good enough to see or touch. I felt completely helpless, like a little girl trapped in a cold war destined to lose the battle. I was in a war with an opponent I loved and hated all at the same time, and the enemy was my mother!

After I started school, my brother and I experienced abuse on another level. Our restrictions started to extend to our bath time; we could only take a bath once a week. As I think about it, we probably always had the same routine; however I became greatly aware of it because I started attending school. Anything that caused you to stand out in an odd way with kids at school opened the door to a whole other world of pain, and having a foul body odor was no exception.

I think I was in the first or second grade when I really started to notice our bizarre bathing habits. I would be given a bath in the same dirty water that my brother took a bath in before me. The water would have a green tint with scum ring around the tub. My mother would scrub my body so hard it would hurt. It felt as if she was trying to rub the skin off of my entire body. I would cry and say "Ouch, that hurts" but that did not make a difference. She would keep right on scrubbing my entire my body without ever stopping. It was like I never said a word. After each bath my mother would lay me on her hard twin size bed and put all sorts of chemicals in my private areas. She would also put rubbing alcohol in my private parts and it would burn really bad. As I lied there staring at the ceiling, I wished I could disappear forever to escape that long lasting burning pain that would sometimes linger for days, especially when I went to use the bathroom. During that time, bathing myself or brushing my own teeth was simply out of the question.

One time I can recall when she cleaned my ears so hard that I cried even after the bath was over. I felt like my ears were going to bleed. Then one time, she cleaned my ears with a Q-tip so deep that the tip got stuck in my ear, and I had to go to the hospital to get it out and stop the bleeding. I remember sitting in the emergency room thinking, "man, my mama is being a very mean lady and I wish I could make her stop."

Even though I got one bath a week, usually on Sunday mornings, just before Sunday school, I dared not complain. After all, I clearly remembered the results of the kitchen protest. So, I figured one day a week of bathing was much better than none.

You see life was painfully bizarre in my house, because my mother suffered from mental illness! She was a born-again believer, baptized in the Name of Jesus and filled with the Holy Ghost. Yet, my mother was diagnosed with developmental delays and "Schizophrenia" which can be marked by extreme mood changes, energy levels, disorganized behavior, and paranoid or unrealistic thoughts. Although adults with Schizophrenia may behave normally in some aspects between episodes of extreme emotion, it is unpredictable what will trigger a manic or hypo manic episode and how long it will last.

In times past, I think the church felt that once you got saved the adverse conditions in your life were instantly over, and that you were immediately delivered from everything. But in my own secret world, I knew that was not the truth. By no means does it negate the power of God. God can do anything, even after we are saved, we are to go on to perfection by the daily renewal of our minds. My mom attended church all the time, but my mom's mind was still in the process of being healed!

CHAPTER TWO

Innocence Interrupted

Suffer the little children to come unto me, and forbid them not: for of such is the kingdom of God.

Mark 10:14

I must give you advanced warning; this chapter contains the painful truth of the sexual abuse that I endured as a child. Some of the content may seem graphic or perhaps to some, maybe even offensive. But, I know by the power of God the truth must be told that others may be set free. The devil hides in the dark secrets of our lives. However, the light of God drives the darkness OUT!

When I was approximately seven-years-old, my mother had a mental breakdown and she was admitted to the psychiatric unit of our local hospital. I am not sure what triggered her episode, but I remember having to go stay with my grandparents on my mother's side as a result of her hospitalization.

My grandmother Evelyn raised a lot of her grandchildren and most of them were older boys. My grandmother is a great woman of God. She possesses the heart of God and really does care about the wellbeing of all her family. Many nights and mornings I would hear Grandma Evelyn crying out to God to save her family, and thanking God for everything He had done. My grandfather, whose nickname was Junior (Jr.) was also a wonderful God fearing person.

My grandparents gave my brother and me a loving place to live when my mother was away in the hospital. I will always love, and appreciate them from the bottom of my heart for caring for us. However, even in a loving home, great hurt and pain can occur. I learned that first hand. Sad to say, it was at my Grandma Evelyn's home where I was sexually molested by my older, male cousins.

Eugenia Rollins

I vividly remember the first time it happened. My grandparents had gone to bed, and somehow I was alone with one of my older cousins watching television in the eat-in kitchen. Like I mentioned earlier, I was only seven-years-old and my cousin was a teenager. Let me take this moment to clearly state that I do not blame my grandparents for anything that happened to me. Nonetheless, one thing that I firmly believe is that children should be monitored on a continual basis. I feel that it is especially important when there are older boys living with younger girls. If parents and guardians keep a watchful eye, they can catch signs of inappropriate behavior.

Unfortunately, the abuse was not a single occurrence. I guess once my cousin shared his story, I then became the target for some of my other cousins as well. I experienced everything from fingers being inserted to my private area to attempted penetration. My cousins may have thought that they were having fun with me. However, in reality they were destroying my life, or so it would seem! Not only were they hurting me physically, they were creating emotional damages that only God and time could heal.

The sexual abuse occurred primarily when Grandma Evelyn had left the house, and my grandfather JR would be gone for a short time or when he was asleep. Although, I was totally unaware that it was wrong for them to be sexually abusing me; I can remember going into the bathroom to urinate feeling scared and confused about the sexual experience I knew I was about to have. I know this may sound crazy, but with the rejection I felt from the kids at school, the attention my cousins gave me made me feel special. I felt like I was gaining their love and friendship by allowing these actions to take place. After all, I felt NO ONE liked me at school; even the teachers were paid to deal with me.

One time in particular, one of my cousins asked to perform another inappropriate sexual act on me, and I did it because he offered me a piece of bubble gum. However, I really said yes because I wanted his love and acceptance. When he finished, I got that piece of pink bubble gum. But, little did I know that I was selling my soul for virtually nothing! One of the lies, my cousins started telling me to continue their demonic acts was: "If you tell, you will get in big trouble too!"

To this day, I can still remember that piece of pink bubble gum and I wish I had thrown it back in his face, then ran and told my grandmother everything. But, I believed the lies about getting in trouble, and I was afraid that my grandmother would be mad at me for some other offense that I had done while she was away. It's amazing the mental traps the enemy sets in our minds.

Another time around Christmas, my grandma Evelyn was in her room, and my cousin and I were in the kitchen, when he started molesting me. I let him do want he wanted because that was one of the only ways he or any of my other cousins would play with me. But this time we got caught!!!! My grandma Evelyn came into the room and saw me rushing to pull up my pants. At that point, she took me in the other bedroom and asked me if I had allowed my cousin to touch me? My answer to her was NO!!!!! The lies and the secrets had taken a strong hold on my life.

Grandma Evelyn never said anything else about it, and the molestation continued. One of the most horrible things about sexual abuse is the fact that it confuses the victim! I know it confused me. As human beings, we instinctively respond to each other's touch. This means that the victim can start to enjoy the acts of abuse because it feels good. That is the deception of the devil. I (the victim) felt shame and guilt, like I was to blame. But, I speak by the power of God, to all who are reading this book right now and have experienced the same type of molestation. You are not to blame! You are an innocent victim of the other person's sickness. And even though your life may have been interrupted by the tragedy of molestation, your life does not have to be destroyed!

By the power of God, you can be healed, saved, and set free!

CHAPTER THREE

When the Bad Outweighs the Good

If the previous chapter offended you, I deeply apologize. Please know that it is not my intent to offend or hurt anyone. But I think something happens to a person, especially to a child when the bad experiences of life vastly outweigh the good ones. For me, a prison cell was created, a cell that only the key of TRUTH can unlock.

Before I continue with the story of my life, I must state that not all of my childhood experiences were bad. Let me explain further.

The Salvation of Genie

I can remember being approximately four-years-old when after our meals, my brother and I would go directly upstairs to our mom's bedroom and watch cartoons for most of the day. We would laugh as we sat on the gray tiled floor on pillows from the couch.

When my mom was in a good mood, from either being on the phone or enjoying a television show, we would be allowed to go out into the hall and play. We used to love to play church and house.

My brother was usually the preacher, he preached from a small blue Bible, or an old tore up medium sized one. He would stand up at the old off white banister that overlooked the flight of stairs that I sat on as he preached. He would preach so hard that he would sweat.

One of his favorite things to say was, "One Lord, One Faith, and One Baptism." It was actually one of the key verses we learned at church on Sundays. I played the church mother, and my one doll with thinning hair served as my child. I would read the scriptures from the steps that we used as our church pews. When our fake services were over, we would go dunk our faces in cold water in the bathroom face bowel and say we got baptized.

27

Eugenia Rollins

When my mother was in an extra good mood, which we could tell by her smiling face and willingness to share her candy, my brother would get to go outside in the back of our house to play on the shattered glass filled basketball court with the other boys. That type of life was all that we knew, so that broken down basketball court was heaven to us.

Sometimes I would go to visit Ms. Bee, a senior citizen that lived behind us on a crime infested block. Ms. Bee's house was very small and crowed with many things that spoke of her history. She had many black and white pictures, glass antiques, and I remember her home always smelling like mothballs and Bengay. However, she was one of the sweetest little ladies.

As I reminisce, I can recollect that she had trouble walking and standing. I'm sure her body was filled with aches and pains; nevertheless she would make cakes and other snacks for me to eat.

She would also let me play "beautician." Although I probably tangled it up once or twice, she always allowed me to comb and braid her hair anyway.

Ms. Bee would sometimes talk about her kids and how one day she wanted to get out of the housing projects. She always hoped that her adult children would come and get her. I could tell it made her a little sad, but she never gave up on what she wanted. I really enjoyed being with Ms. Bee. Those were our fun times as I can recall.

As I continue to think about it, I can truly say that there were happy times in my life. But what happens when the bad experiences in life greatly outweigh the good ones?

I remember for many years my brother, mother, and I all slept in the same full sized bed. The bed was raised very high off of the tiled floor; and even though I was very young I slept on the edge of the bed. One night I fell out of bed, and actually rolled underneath it. The fall broke my shoulder bone.

That one event seemed to be the start of my non-ending drama. Child Protective Services were notified and the courts took us out of my mother's custody for nine months.

Although I was only four going on five-years-old, I still slightly recall being in the courtroom. I was sitting on someone's lap in the audience behind the witness stand, and the judge said we were going to my daddy's house. My mother started crying. I felt like something bad had happened but I could not explain what was going on. So, to our daddy's house we went.

My dad and his parents (Grandpa Snoop and grandma Leathia) lived together in a gray single story three bedroom house. While staying with my dad, I can remember hating to get my hair combed by my Grandma Leathia. She would make me sit down on my assigned pillow and would comb all the naps out without mercy. When I would start wiggling around, she would say, "Girl, be still or you 'bout to get hit wit dis comb."

I used to sit at the kitchen table for hours because I refused to eat the food sometimes. I recall this one time my grandmother cooked some chicken for breakfast. The food smelled great, like we were in my great grandparent's house in the south. However for some odd reason, I did not want the chicken. So, I put it in the trash.

I could not believe my eyes; grandma Leathia got the chicken out the trash and told me to sit at that round cherry wood table until I ate all of that chicken.

Because I refused to eat it, it was after dinnertime when I was finally allowed to get up from the table. I had sat there all day long. On many other occasions I would eat so slow that it would be lunchtime and I was still eating breakfast. I didn't really know what the problem was, the food or me!

When I was not at the kitchen table, my brother and I had these big pillows that we sat on to watch the "soaps" (day-time television drama series) with my Grandma Leathia. Without question, the soaps were a time that we knew we had to be quiet. If we weren't, we had to go play in the back room or outside in the yard.

Once again, I had my assigned pillow. It was red and blue checkerboard patterned pillow. And as I remember, I sat on that pillow a whole lot.

Sometimes after the daily mealtime war and getting my "naps" combed, I did not want to play outside. So, I became a fan of *All My Children*, one of the most popular soaps at the time.

While living at my daddy's house, my brother started Kindergarten. I had to stay home with my grandma, grandpa and the dog. My dad had to work. I recall being happy even though all I did was watch the soaps and play outside with my brother sometimes when he would come home from school.

Watching my brother prepare for school every morning made feel like school was so much fun. I wanted to go with him so bad that would I cry and beg my dad to please let me go too. But his reply was "not yet, you will start school when you go back to live with your mama." Little did I know that time was right at hand.

The time my brother and I spent at my dad and grandparent's house was pretty good. But again I ask, what happens when the bad experiences in a person's life greatly outweigh the good ones?

Nine months had quickly elapsed, and back to momma's house we went. Absolutely nothing had changed. This time because my brother and I were a little older, and had just come from a structured environment, we knew that things were still very bizarre with our mom. But sadly, there was nothing we could do about it.

We both noticed that at my daddy's house we were allowed to take baths on a regular basis. And at my dad's, we could change clothes daily and go outside to play.

Painfully, at my mother's house that was not the case. We had no freedom! We were totally confined!

We were only allowed in my mother's room. We had another bedroom but we were absolutely forbidden to enter it. Of course, we went to the bathroom. But, we could never enter the kitchen! We could only eat in the dining-room area that was not attached to the kitchen.

Our home had what you might call a family room of sorts. It was located in the lower level of our home. It was there that my brother and I now slept. We could sleep and talk there and even sometimes play quietly when my mother was asleep.

To me our house felt more like a museum that had many off-limit rooms and displays. I could never understand why, after all we were poor and in the projects. Nobody wanted what we owned!

Our playtime was even limited! Basically, we did nothing but go to church and walk to Grandma Evelyn's house. Thankfully, Grandma Evelyn's house provided some short-lived relief from my mother, because we got to play outside when my mother was occupied with other people.

During this time whenever my dad attempted to visit my brother and me, it was under hostile terms. I can remember my daddy riding his bike over to our house in the blazing summer heat to see us, on many occasions. My mom would not allow him or us the privilege of spending time with each other. As she saw him approaching, she would call the police or just not open the door.

I remember one hot and sunny Saturday morning; my dad came over riding his bike to visit. He had completed his newspaper route for the day. As we got excited to see our dad I remember looking out of the window only to see the police driving up at the same time. My mother had called the police on my dad because she simply did not want him to see us. My dad left. After that episode his visits were few and very between.

This made me feel even angrier with my mother. I just could not understand why she would push away our dad especially when all he wanted to do was visit his children, he had come to know and love!

However, in the late summer, right before the start of school my mother would allow my dad to take us shopping for new school clothes each year. Even though she still did not let him visit us!

Things that make you go Hummmmm???? But then when school started, she would not allow us to wear the clothes that he had worked hard to purchase. Our hopes were let down year after year, as we longed to wear our new clothes to school like the other kids, but nothing ever changed!

I can only describe it like this: Life at my mother's house was Hell on Earth.

With so much pinned up anger and resentment, it was not long before my brother and I started to display progressively worse behavioral problems.

For fun, we used to play on the phone and call cabs to the neighbor's house across the street. Then, we would peak out the window when the cab arrived to watch everyone get upset as they argued over the requested cab.

We also used to call for pizza delivery to the next-door neighbor's house. We would laugh, as the pizza man and our neighbor fought over the order, and who was going to pay for the pizza.

We would also hit each other's pencils until one of our pencils broke. That type of mischief had become our fun.

Often times we would be openly wayward: Before school we would walk down to the corner store to buy candy, when we were supposed to be going directly to school. The little walk was important to me, because we would laugh and talk about how we were going to get liberated from my mother one day.

My brother and I also used to chat about how the other kids looked nice and how we didn't. Though it was very rough, we depended on each other for laughter. Just being together made our living hell so much better! Little did I know that before long that would change!

When my brother and mother kept struggling over his freedom, he finally got the attention of the Child Protective Services once again. I think his teacher or someone must have noticed that he had become extremely depressed. I therefore, had to watch helplessly, as by brother was hospitalized to get some mental rest. After his release, my brother became "A Ward of the State" and then he was gone for good. I got to see him, but he never came back to the "Cell Block". Now, at the age of eleven, I was in my prison cell alone!

I became a mental mess. Even though I knew my brother was in a healthier place, I still felt abandoned by him.

Next, I had to watch my mom go from awful to worse especially when she started to act bizarre with the people in our community. They would call her "the crazy lady" and treat her like a second-class citizen when we went to places like stores, doctors' offices and even to church sometimes. Yet, somehow, I felt responsible for protecting the same mother that continued hurting me. I would look after her no matter what. Only for her to turn around and treat me like yesterday's trash! I must explain this a bit more!

Before my brother became a Ward of the State, both of us suffered the same abuse, but it was worse for him, because he was a boy.

We were not allowed to bathe or use deodorant except on Sundays. So you can imagine how we must have smelled. We both had to wear the same dirty, smelly clothes to school every day.

Therefore, we were both teased and picked on by the other children at school. From the time I started kindergarten until graduation I was subjected to my classmate's cruelty.

Children can be painfully honest. They just say what they feel, be it good or bad. I was the child that happened to be on the receiving end of their evil deeds and their cruel but honest words. Well, at least my brother had escaped!

Alone to fend for myself, I felt really powerless, ashamed, angry, and confused. I knew this was not the way life was supposed to be, but there was nothing I could say or do to make my mother treat me any better.

I felt like I was in prison inside my own home and inside of another prison of sorts which was the increasingly violent housing projects. Lastly, the worst of all prisons was my school. I had a 12 year sentence to complete with summer breaks. Now, how can a person, especially a child, survive all of that?

After a while, I became tormented by my own negative thoughts. With no help in sight, I just felt left alone to die! Unfortunately by this time in my life, I had also experienced the sexual abuse that I shared in the previous chapter.

I was still a child, but I had lived a lifetime of bad experiences!

It felt like no one could see me, not my teachers, peers, or even my church. The normal things that a young girl needs to thrive successfully I was deprived of. There were no hugs, kisses, or any love from my mother. Little by little, I was increasingly losing my identity.

The arguments with my mother started to turn violent, as I constantly told her I needed to bathe and use deodorant on other days besides Sunday. I would also insist that I needed to wear different clothes other than dirty ones she selected for me. She even decided when to pass out my sanitary napkins, which usually was when she felt I needed one.

With a combination of all of this, who would not have a strong body odor if they only bathed one day out of a week? So, I would just go around "stinking" in dirty clothes, with the exception of Sundays. Also the teasing of my classmates used to echo in my mind as I tried to sleep at night.

So again I ask, what happens when the bad experiences in a person's life immeasurably outweigh the good ones?

At this point in my life, I hated my mother for being so cruel towards me. Our arguments were so hurtful, as they seemed to last for an eternity. Once during an argument, I hit my mother out of pure frustration. It was one of those days when she was screaming that I did not need a bath. However, in my mind I could hear the kids making fun of me as they always did, and before I knew it I had struck her hard.

Hitting my mother made me feel good and bad at the same time. I was sorry after I hit her but I just did not know what else to do!

The church had taught me that I could go to hell for being disrespectful to my parents. I really wanted to be saved! But, with no one to help me I felt like hell was destined to be my home!

After a while, I just stopped caring. I started fighting and doing evil and mean things to my mother just to make me feel better.

Now here's the answer to the question about, what happens when the bad experiences in a person's life greatly outweigh the good ones? The good in that person OFTEN TURNS BAD AND UNFORTUNATELY, MINE DID!

CHAPTER FOUR

Help, Save Me from Myself!

If you are finding these chapters overwhelming to bear, please hang on and don't stop reading. I have heard it said, "It's the darkest, right before the dawn." We sing a song in my church entitled: *To the Uttermost, Jesus Saves.* The uttermost means the worse or extreme scenario. Well, to me, my situation was the uttermost!

After enduring years of sexual abuse from my cousins, another family member started molesting me. However, this time I was older, around eleven or twelve, and I knew what was happening was

WRONG! The abuse occurred for such a long time, and not knowing how to stop it, something inside of me gave in to it. Before I knew it, my body craved to be touched.

At that point in my life, I learned that my body could bring me pleasurable sensations. But those same experiences were causing me to feel guilt, shame, anger, embarrassment, and hurt. Although I felt completely dirty after each occurrence, I could not control my longing for it to happen again. I enjoyed the feeling of being wanted and important to somebody in life, even though it was from my abuser. In reality, they did not care and were being used by Satan to attempt to destroy me. I was only being used for their own perversions.

At such a young age I was not able to mentally process what my body was feeling, the good, the bad, and the ugly. As a result, I struggled with my thoughts and emotions in secret. I knew it felt nice, but why was it nice when I was told it was wrong? I hated it, but liked it, and then I hated myself for not knowing the difference between the two.

Suffering with all of these extreme emotions and not knowing how to get them out, led to results that were disastrous!

At the age of thirteen, I was finally allowed to shower alone. It was there in the shower that I created my own personal torture chamber. I would scrub so hard that sometimes my body would bleed. I wanted to wash away every nasty touch that made me feel like a whore, since the age of seven.

Sometimes, I would scrub so hard that it would hurt for me to walk or sit. Physically, I would be in a great deal of pain, but when I hurt myself I felt better. It was as if I was giving myself the punishment I well deserved!

Anger, rage, and confusion boiled inside of me because I did not know how to stop hurting. I got this uncontrollable urge to hurt myself in any way possible. I would scratch myself until I would bleed, bite the insides of my jaws until they bled, and somehow find a way to do harm to my body. Hurting my body brought sweet relief.

One time I remember my mother and I got into a verbal fight over me wanting to take a bath and use some deodorant. After we fought and I lost, I went into the bathroom; I looked in the mirror and began to scratch my face so intensely that people thought a cat had scratched up my face.

In today's terms counselors and psychiatrists would call my behavior "cutting." Cutting is described as an outward expression of the internal emotion of rage, anger taken out on one's own body. I knew cutting was wrong, but I became addicted to the relief cutting brought. For about seven to ten years I struggled intensely with cutting.

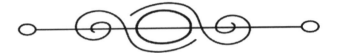

This is such a painful part of my past to open up and share. But I know that by sharing my story I am helping someone to get free. And I am setting myself free as well. I simply refuse to wear the garments of shame and embarrassment anymore.

The truth is, some of the people we work with, worship with, a family member, or maybe even you, have had similar battles. Perhaps you or someone you know has not had the courage to face their monsters. But please know that you are not alone! Whatever it is that you deal with that banishes you to a secret prison of pain, God sees it, and wants to set you FREE! And for the record, people that attend church and participate in various ministries are included in our group!

I am what some people would call a "pew baby." I was raised in church from birth. My mother took my brother and I to church every Sunday, Monday, Wednesday, and Friday. During some special weeks throughout the year we went to church every day. Yet, I dealt with these issues.

Due to the fact that no one helped me during the sexual abuse and the cutting, I lost all hope sitting right in the church. I knew Jesus was real, but He felt so far away from me. I felt like Jesus was mad at me all the time and I thought that explained my suffering. We were taught that any small infraction made us a candidate for hell. Even if we repented, we would still have to suffer terrible consequences. I felt like God was paying me back. That is the way I understood most of the sermons I heard.

Eugenia Rollins

During my journey through the flames of hell, I rarely missed a Sunday of church. I also attended Bible classes and prayer meetings all of the time. I knew the song: *Yes, Jesus Loves Me* in my mind, but my heart could not receive it.

Occasionally, even in my mid-twenties, I would still feel that intense rage and pain. Consequently, I would turn to cutting (hurting myself), but not in the places that people could see. I found it easy to hide from people, but I could never hide from God!

Although in the past the cutting seemed to bring relief, the older I got, the more tired I became of the devils lies, and the strongholds he had on my mind! I desperately needed to be saved from myself! At prayer meetings, I started asking God to heal and set me free! I will never forget this, one Wednesday afternoon, at noonday Bible study, I knew it was over! Instantly, the urge to "cut" (hurt myself) was GONE! God is so faithful!!!

The Salvation of Genie

My Savior heard my desperate cries and did what no other

human being could do for me; He healed and delivered me from the

inside out. God specializes in situations that man cannot fix!

Eugenia Rollins

CHAPTER FIVE

School Days/My Genesis

It is so important to be whole and complete in every area of your life, because a building can only be as strong as its foundation.

As you have read in the previous chapters, my home life was full of pain, anger and stress. I was like a building whose foundation was filled with tremendous cracks. Anything constructed on such an unstable foundation is destined to crumble.

While my life at home remained broken and splintered, school was no better. Let me start from the beginning.

I attended Carter Elementary School. It was down the street directly across from a factory my brother and I called the "bud plant." I don't know why we gave the company that name. Now that I think about it, we didn't even know what "buds" were. The silly name just seemed to fit.

Well, Carter Elementary was a place where I learned to feel inadequate. I guess you could say from kindergarten until I graduated high school in 1998, I thought I was never going to be as smart as the other kids. And being successful at anything in life certainly would not be an option for me. After all, some teachers, the kids in my classes and countless other circumstances at home told me so.

I can clearly remember being called terrible names like, "yoooou are ugly", "your clothes stink", "hey you peed on yourself", "four eyes", among many other words. It's amazing how such painful memories can haunt you for a lifetime. I can still hear the emphasis they placed on the word yoooou. It seemed to ring throughout eternity.

What's more devastating are the cracks in my foundation of life that I could feel occurring from each experience.

This torture literally ran from kindergarten until I graduated from high school. Thank God that some years were a little bit better

Eugenia Rollins

than others. Consequently, after being teased so long, it became a part of my educational path, and as common as paper, pencils and my textbooks.

In kindergarten I had a wonderful teacher. She was very patient with the class as we attempted to master basic skills like cutting and pasting. It seemed all of the kids were doing well, with the exception of me. Cutting and pasting was not a skill I mastered with ease. Later on I found out why. After numerous medical tests, I was diagnosed as having mild "cerebral palsy," a dysfunction that affected my motor skills among various other basic functions.

That was certainly not a good start to my academic foundation.

I have vivid memories of first grade. I recall that none of the kids wanted to touch me, or anything I owned. I felt like I had a deadly plague that could kill a population. I was really one of the "untouchables."

My homework papers never got graded. Literally!! The kids would always drop them on the floor and in some cases refuse to pick up my papers until the teacher demanded that they pick it up. This made me feel like I was bad and nasty. I could not understand what I did wrong or what I had that made my paper diseased. I felt like being me was what was wrong. The teacher would be teaching and I remember not being able to recall anything she would say. Mrs. Jefferson would ask me questions and I would just snap out of a daze. I daydreamed, looking out at the "bud plant" for most of the day.

In the second grade, I encountered a whole new set of circumstances but a very valuable, lifelong blessing came my way. At church, I met my best and only friend for many years. We stayed friends for many years. We remain best friends to this day. And although we did not attend the same schools, she helped ease some of the pain that school brought me.

Everything was normal for a little while, and then I started to miss a significant amount of school because my mother got a new boyfriend. We stayed at his small sixth floor apartment so much that I missed many days of school.

My mother's boyfriend was physically handicapped. He could not walk and used a wheelchair to get around.

One day he and my mother got into a serious argument. They were screaming at each other and he was cussin' her out. My mother said we were leaving because they were so mad at each other.

As we got on the stainless steel elevator, they were still screaming at each other. My mother stood in the corner of the elevator and I stood in the back next to her. He got in the elevator and continued to cuss her out. He then rolled up to hit her and before I knew it, she had grabbed me and put me in front of her to block the hit. But God protected. His swing missed me and I was not harmed.

I felt I had no protector for my life. But I recall the scripture that states; "When my father and mother forsake me, then the Lord will take me up." Boy was I a living witness to God's precious promises.

Meanwhile back at school, that is, the days that I actually went to school, my teacher yelled at me. Mrs. Sims would yell at me to stay focused most of the day. It was very embarrassing to be yelled at in front of the other children, but on top of that the teacher assigned another student in the class to yell at me every time I got off task. The girl would yell out loud, "Genie get busy."

My teacher never asked me what was going on. She just assumed that I was slow. In the second grade is when the sexual abuse began in my life. I felt confused, angry, and hurt. Consequently, I failed the second grade. I was embarrassed because everyone knew that I failed. The class lists were posted in each class's window so students and parents would know what class to go to on the first day. My name was on second grade list again and all my other classmates were on the third grade list.

One time, in particular the teacher said in front of the whole class, as she stood in the back talking with the gym teacher, "Dang, Eugenia you stink, do you ever take a bath?" I cannot express to you how I felt in that moment. I wished for that moment that I could have been smaller than the dirt on the floor. The other students in the class heard her and started to laugh. One of the students that sat by me laughed so hard she was told to stop.

Death seemed better than life. Think for a moment; have you ever seen a young child having a tantrum because he or she could not have their way? Well internally I was having a tantrum that only I could see. This fit of anger and rage was due to the enormous amount of confusion and lack of stability that filled my life.

Thank God, the third grade was one of my better years. My mother and Edward broke up. My school attendance was better and somehow I made the honor roll.

In the fourth grade, the overall rejection of my classmates continued. I remember being in gym class and being embarrassed to change my clothes because I felt like I was so ugly. All the girls would be in the bathroom talking and no one would say anything to me. I was too afraid to say anything to them. I would go in the stinky, graffiti filled stall to change my clothes and hope that the gym class would go fast. In gym class, I was always picked last for every game.

However, due to fact that I had no friends at school, I had a lot of spare time on my hands. And with that time I turned my attention to books. That year I discovered I had a true passion for reading.

Once in my class, the teacher asked me to read from my science book to the class, as we sat in the circle and I read; I did so well I shocked myself. I was able to read fluently with a loud strong voice. Books then became my constant companion. I would read during any free moment I had. I read books, newspapers, magazines, and whatever else I could get my hands on. I read the Bible too.

In the fifth grade the kids still taunted me, which made it difficult for me to stay focused. But this time, I had a teacher who was observant to the situation. My teacher made my permanent seat in the corner up by her desk. I hated that seat but I did get my work done. Unlike some of the instructors I had in the past, I felt like this teacher really cared about me.

By the sixth grade, the molestation that had taken place earlier in my life was over. On the outside looking in, things would seem to be much more normal in my life. While maintaining my church attendance and creating a façade that all was well, I almost had a major mental breakdown. I wanted to just stop everything. In reality, my life was getting harder.

My family was enrolled in family counseling to help my brother with his tribulations and concerns. The counselor really made an honest attempt to breakthrough to me during each session but my will was unbreakable.

I had built a wall high as high as the Sears Tower and as thick as ten full sized dictionaries. I had learned it was safer to keep things on the inside.

After many attempts in many sessions she stopped trying because I was not going to say anything. As I write this section I am starting to feel some emotions. I cannot clearly describe these feelings; it feels like a combination of fear, sadness, and tears that a child would cry. To that adult who may be secretly struggling with childhood pain, I want to say that it is okay. God can make you whole. I have found that writing has helped me to get it out; you may find other positive outlets to get it out.

One good thing that happened; I was selected to audition for a visual and performing arts school for my vocal ability. That was such an honor.

In the seventh grade I finally found out what had been wrong with my mother.

The doctor said to me, "your mother has a chemical imbalance in the brain that is called schizophrenia." Schizophrenia is defined as, *"delusions, false beliefs, not explained by religion or culture, which are maintained in spite of evidence to the contrary."*(pg.71) Schizophrenia can be displayed through hallucinations, disorganized speech, and disorganized behavior and manic or hypo manic episodes that can last for various spans of time, or many other symptoms.

The diagnoses made me feel more hopeless than ever before. What was I supposed to do to help her get well? There were many days when I felt like skipping school. However, God sent two angels in the form of two ladies from my church. Their names were Mother Jones and Rachel Hooper, they would drive past and I would change my mind every time I saw them.

Mother Jones and Rachel Hooper were very valuable assets for me during middle school and my freshman year of high school. Mother Jones would talk to me about doing right and planting good seeds. Mother Jones really took time to know me by allowing me to just say how I felt. Mother Jones and I would talk on the phone often and she would let my best friend and I come to her house to hang out. We would talk about God but she would also talk to us about life. Mother Jones loved to hear about what happened to us at school and how we were doing with planting good seeds in our classmates.

Mother Jones was my girl. I could tell her anything within reason and she would listen to me and not judge my feelings. Plus, sometimes when my mother would punish me by not allowing me to attend church events or services, she would tell her to let me go to church. Sometimes it would work other times it did not work at all. Mother Jones passed away when I was in high school. To keep her memory alive, for many years I had a teddy bear I named after her. I also wrote special poem in her memory.

Mother Jones Poem

Mother Jones was here but now she's gone,
She left sweet memories to carry on,
Through her dark hours and her nights the God in her still shined
Bright,
Mother Jones went out of her way to help others because God
Commanded that we love one another,
Though this may seem as an hour of sorrow,
God promises if we
Live right we will see her tomorrow,
Now Mother Jones is resting safely in Gods arms and nothing or no one
can do her any harm.
(Dedicated to my friend on September 22, 1995)

Rachel Hooper was another asset to me because she would give me hugs. When she hugged me I did not feel untouchable or rejected. During eighth grade I had a lot of face-to-face meetings with my pastor about the issues that were going on in my home.

Despite these meetings, my mother continued to make me wear dirty clothes to school, and I was still only allowed one bath a week.

As year progressed I just stopped talking. I was very quiet in school and at church I would go through the motions of being well. It got so bad that one day my mother and I got into a fight again over not being able to take a bath or use deodorant. This was one of those days I did not feel very fresh. I just could not take it any more so I started being real mean and hateful to her. I started beating the door and cussing at her to the point I really lost control. I think I hit her in the chest.

Before school, I started going over to my friend's house to change clothes so that the kids would not make fun of me. Also, one of the women in the church would bring me deodorant whenever I told her that my mother had me on a deodorant strike. Sister Love really cared about me but she did not know how to help except for letting me come to her house to stay the night sometimes. She also brought me the basics for good hygiene that I had to hide so that my mother would not confiscate them from me. Her showing me that kind of love meant so much. At school, I would wear my friend's clothes all day then at the end of last period I changed back into my clothes. One day I almost got caught. My mother came to school like three minutes after I had changed my clothes. This was a very close call, but Jesus was looking out for me.

During my freshmen year of high school my mother would come to the school randomly. I hated it so bad that I would literally run from her. She would be in the crowd yelling my name and I would be gone. My peers used to call her mean names like, "crazy lady."

Throughout the era of my childhood it was very uncommon in my church to deal with child abuse, mental illness, deliverance or inner healing. For every problem the answer was to pray and God would work it out. But I found out that God uses people.

Some of the saints would take us to the store and buy me things; they also attempted to encourage my mother to buy me things. My mother rarely bought me clothes or anything. My clothes generally were hand me downs or a church member would buy them for me. On one occasion, my mother bought me a blouse and a skirt with the money I earned from a summer job. When we went to the stores and I asked for something, she would say, "I buy you food and toiletries that's all you need" how funny was it that she would buy toiletries but rarely allow me use them?

I don't think it was her not buying me clothes that bothered me, but it was the fact that I knew she did not want to buy anything for me. At school, I saw a lot of the students wearing nice name brand clothes, like Fubu, Nike, Guess Jeans, Cross Colors, and all the other trends on the 90's. Personally, I felt I looked so bad that I did not have the confidence to reach out to my peers.

This was the foundation on which my life was built; a foundation filled with cracks from a hard life. *Anything constructed on such an unstable foundation is destined to crumble,* and in the years ahead I would experience that!

CHAPTER SIX

Losing the Battle but Winning the War

Nobody wants to suffer! As a matter of fact I think most people; especially Christians want to go through life on a flowery bed of ease. However, I have found an old church saying to be very true. You can never have a testimony without the test!

It was near the end of my freshmen year of high school, I had taken all that I could take of the mental, verbal, and physical abuse of living with my mom. I was exhausted from caring for her while she treated me like trash!

I guess you could say I was on the edge, like a dead man walkin'. My emotional mask was cracking. I hated getting up every day and I started to desire death more than life. It was becoming harder to smile beyond all the pain, anger, and rejection.

One day, my father drove over to visit me and as we sat outside in his red two-door old school LaBaron, I stared at the cloudy sky and told him that I was at my breaking point! As I poured out what was left of my heart, I stated "If I did not get out soon, he would be reading about me in the newspaper for murder!" I was serious.

I became so enraged that I envisioned pushing my mother down a flight of stairs, throwing scalding hot pans on her, and lastly overdosing her on her medicine or cold medication.

I needed peace like I needed air to breath, and I needed it NOW! As I pondered my options, I came to a conclusion that there was only one solution. One of us was going to have to die! Kill or be killed. It had come down to that. The mental and emotional pressure was mounting to the point of no return.

Finally, the day came; I was eating dinner alone at the table after a long hard day at school. As usual, my mother started fussing about nothing. I longed for her to be quiet. All I wanted was a little peace. As she became more and more aggressive, I could not stand it anymore; I just blew up and went completely off. Suddenly, I found myself holding a sharp butcher knife attempting to stab my mother in the chest!

Can you believe it? Looking back, I can't! The woman, who gave me life, hurt me so bad that now I was going to take hers.

It all happened so quick, I really do not think I was conscious of what I was doing. Despite my fleshly desire to kill my mother, God said, "NO!" Needless to say, my aim was off and my feeble attempt was to no avail. My mother was not harmed at all.

Well, someone still had to die. Kill or be killed, I reminded myself. So, if I could not kill my mother, the next best thing was for me to try to kill myself.

I had the same butcher knife in my right hand, while I attempted to cut my left wrist open so I would bleed to death. This was like an out of body experience. As I sat there, I gritted my teeth and proceeded to take the knife to my wrist. Again, God said, "NO!"

My right arm became hard as a rock, therefore I could not move. I sat in a frozen trance for about three to four minutes. By the power of God, no one died that day.

A few days after that incident, I found myself enlisting the help of my family and friends to escape my captivity, so I asked for help to run away.

By this point, school was out and the summer break was just beginning. I knew that I had to go or the next time she would die without question. I told my daddy to get me a ticket to another city so that I could get as far away as I could. Somehow, my aunt was contacted in another city and she was told that I had a bus ticket to go see her. That was the truth. My father had bought me a one way ticket. Luckily for me, my aunt did not want me to ride the bus so she came and got me.

Now the getaway, the day unfolded like this, it was a warm but cloudy Saturday morning. One of my other aunts had finally convinced my mother that I could stay home alone. That was very surprising being that in the fourteen years of my life I had never been trusted to stay alone. My aunt came by and took my mother shopping. When my mother left for the store, I got all my clothes together and put what little I had in bags. It was like a battle against the clock, my heart palpitated as I went looking for bags and clothes. Since I was confined to only the dining room and her bedroom, I did not know where anything was. I ran up and down the brown tiled flight of stairs trying to gather my thoughts and say good-bye all at the say time. It was like a bittersweet dream was coming true, my other aunt came around the corner and got me. I came out the house with my two plastic shopping bags filled with clothes and I left. By the time my mother came home from the store, I was gone and already on the highway. I did what I had to do to survive.

I knew that my mother would be very hurt and angry but I did not know what else to do. So at the age of fourteen I moved out my mother's house never to return.

Although I escaped, I felt like I had lost the battle! But, the war for my salvation was far from over.

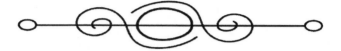

Once I arrived at my aunt's house I was very happy, nervous, afraid, confused and lastly hurt all at the same time. I remember the first couple of days being very problematic internally for me. I could hardly eat, sleep or make very small decisions for myself. I was shaking on the inside. It felt like I had the chills but I was not cold. Although I felt I had no other choice, I still wondered if I had done the right thing because of my mother's issues. I worried about her taking care of herself? I also wondered if I would be able to function without my mother. After all, she taught me very few life skills. What would the church members say about me? Who would understand or believe my story? What would happen if the court got involved like they did with my brother? The list went on and on.

As the summer progressed, I calmed down and started to have fun with my cousins, aunt and uncle.

During that summer a pen pal/mentor that had kept in touch with me from a youth camp years before, invited me to go to

Truth Ministries' youth camp (a Christian summer camp). I was extremely hesitant to go for a few reasons. For one, I was informed that the girls had to wear skirts. I did not own many skirts that were appropriate for this camp experience. Secondly, I would hardly know anyone. Despite my concerns, I went anyway. My cousin went as well.

Upon arriving on the campgrounds in Zanesville, Ohio, I was amazed to see so many young people wanting to praise the Lord. I got there and experienced the presence of the Lord. The power of God really began to minister to me. It was during this camp that I was so deeply touched by the power of God that I was on the ground, crying out to God for some real help. At that point, I had envisioned my funeral and all the people that would attend. I had never experienced seeing anything like that unless I was dreaming.

TM Youth Camp was one of the best weeks of my life. TM Camp gave me the desire to go from rules and rituals to a real relationship with God. I felt connected to God as never before. On the campgrounds, I could feel myself exhaling the mental and emotional pressure that had been built up over most of my life. Also there I did not feel like a reject. People talked to me and sat with me at the different meal times. It was good to be in a place where all I had to do was focus on God and God could finally talk to me! Actually, He had been talking all the time; I wasn't sure just how well I had been listening. After all, I was too busy hearing the voices of my mother and negative schoolmates.

The time that I spent at my uncle and aunt's house was like a safe refuge, but little did I know that it would be a part of my salvation. God had rescued me, right in the nick of time.

I loved my family. They attended church regularly, and they included me in all of their family outings. One of my cousins is very close to my age so we had many things to laugh and talk about, from school to funny family stories. From the time I was very young, I was always told how well my cousin was doing in school and how she was really involved in church. Therefore during my stay, I was blessed to be around one the smartest young ladies that I have ever met (my cousin).

I am forever grateful for the unconditional love they had shown me. My aunt never judged me or preached to me. In her wisdom, she prayed for me and let me go through my healing process. My aunt extended the opportunity for me to go to school with my cousin. Although it was a wonderful opportunity, I declined and decided to go live with my dad, grandparents and brother.

So after that summer I went back to Gary, Indiana to go to school. It is amazing how things came full circle. I had lived with them as a very young child and now as a teenager. The house was cool but it was a totally different set up. Now, everyone was older and living their own lives. At my daddy's house I had freedom, freedom to choose what I wanted to do. Even though, the only things that I did were go to church and to my friend's house who lived down the street. There were some nights that I found myself at home with my grandma Leathia.

My grandmother was a nice lady; however she had many illnesses that sometimes made her irritable. My grandmother always talked to me about getting an education and not having sex as we sat in the living room watching the news in the dark. She had a very special way of talking to me. I felt like she was being harsh, but somehow I knew she had good intentions. I lived in the house with my grandmother for only eight months before she passed away. After her death, I found myself home alone most days after school.

My father worked many long hard hours, and did a superior job of providing for us. We always had food to eat and he would always have extra change to give me to buy snacks. When my father came home from work late at night he would eat and go to sleep on the couch. Every morning he woke me up for school and sometimes cooked me breakfast to make sure I had a meal. Then he drove me to school every day while we listened to the Tom Joyner Morning Show in that old faithful red LaBaron.

If he knew I was not in a good mood, he would stop at the truck stop and buy me some candy. My favorite candies to buy were the Reeses Pieces and Good & Plenty in the purple and white box. I would eat on that all day in my classes. As I reflect on it, we became closer during the times when he would drive me to school. It was so sweet, the way he would wait until I got almost to the door before he drove off, that made me feel like he really cared about me. He always made sure I had bus fare to get back home, because he would be at work.

One early spring day all the students, teachers, and other staff had a rally for "peace in our school and neighborhoods" in the school's auditorium. These Peace Rallies were somewhat common;

we had one each semester. However this one was different, it was the last hour of the day and I was getting my things together and going to the bus stop as usual. Some of the other kids were also at the bus stop when gunshots erupted suddenly. There was no time to run back in the school or really even think. I just started running down the street. As I ran a bullet flew right pass my head. No one got hurt in that shoot out besides one girl that had an asthma attack. I still thank God for keeping me. From that moment on, after school I did not mess around at all, I went straight to my house.

After school my grandfather and brother would be out socializing. Sometimes, my brother would have social events in the basement. I was not allowed to attend due to what would be going on. My brother and his friends would be drinkin', smokin' weed and listening to music, as they call it "chillin' out."

One time on New Year's Eve, my brother and his friends were smokin' weed in the basement, while I was headed off to church. We had what was called a foot washing and communion service. It's a service where men, women, and children assemble themselves together to encourage each other and follow the Biblical example of Jesus washing the disciples' feet as found in *St. John 13*.

As I went into the church, one of the church members thought I was high because I smelled like weed. That night I did have a contact high. My eyes were pink and I was feeling very light headed. Unfortunately, my brother smoked weed very often, which created a smoke cloud that filled my house. Since I was trying so hard to make right choices, I was lonesome most days. I was glad that the summer break was just about over.

When school started back, things had not changed much. The peers from my past still made fun of me and called me ugly. However, one major thing had changed; I was back at school without a mother! It's so crazy, although I had a terrible relationship with my mother, I still desperately longed for what a mother's love should be.

I found myself longing to feel connected, accepted and affirmed. I wanted to feel a mother's love in the worst way. No sister, aunt or cousin, could fulfill the need that I had.

I wondered what it would be like to have someone to share my heart with, without judgment. I wanted someone to do "girly" stuff with. This deep longing led me on a quest to find someone to connect with. I did not care if it was a teacher, church member, or neighbor. I just wanted to experience a mother's love.

While in my search, I found myself at the school library. Also, I hung out at the parent resource center during my lunch hour. Hey, after all maybe there would be a mother in there that I could connect with.

I had no such luck. However, to my amazement I found that there was a prayer group going on. I went every time they had it. I found this group to be enriching and a place where the kids would not talk about me. There, it did not matter what I had on or what I looked like. The focus in the group was praying for God to help our school and its students. There were teachers and parent volunteers in this group as well. The prayer group members became my friends. I was in my senior year of high school, and that was my first time having friends at school.

By the time the president graduated, the prayer group was left in my hands my senior year. That shocked me, but I knew that I enjoyed prayer so I figured this would be a good challenge for me. As a result, the prayer group became my focal point.

The dreadful kids from my past did not upset me anymore, because I had a place where I was connected and accepted.

One of the young ladies in that group is still one of my good friends today. While I was blessed to be president of the prayer group, I was also blessed to see many souls accept Jesus Christ as their personal savior. I witnessed souls being filled with the Holy Spirit. The baptism of the Holy Spirit is a gift from God that comes with the evidence of speaking in other tongues as recorded in the Holy Bible in *Acts Chapter 2*.

I remember one student who was a member of our prayer group. She was a very sweet girl who wanted to learn all she could about God. I began to explain to her about the power of the Holy Ghost, how it is real, and that she could have it if she believed in it. She had already confessed her sins and accepted Jesus Christ as her savior. As we walked down the hall to the area where the woodshop classes were held, she stated that she was ready. Right there at school, she received the Holy Ghost with the evidence of speaking in Heavenly tongues. It was not as hard as I had been trained to think. Seeing her receive the gift of the Holy Ghost really put a spark in me to reach as many people as I could while in school. From that experience I decided to put aside the things I was dealing with. In turn, I really became involved in bringing my peers to God.

Life improved even more when I graduated from high school in 1998. As I walked across the stage, I spoke in my "Heavenly Language" as I cried tears joy! It was over.

As I reflect back on the dreaded day when Satan tried to influence me to kill my mom, he knew that would have been something I could have never forgiven myself for. Also, I could have been sent to prison for the rest of my entire life. Worse yet, if I had succeeded at committing suicide, I could not have asked for God's forgiveness, and would have died in my sins and been eternally lost!

So, I may have lost the battle that day, but God was preparing me to "Win the War!"

CHAPTER SEVEN

Beyond What I Could Have Imagine

And I will do exceeding abundantly above all that you could ask or think!

After graduating from high school, I settled in a new city, Muncie, Indiana. You may wonder how I ended up in a place called Muncie, Indiana.

Well, my cousin Lena, the one that I spoke of in earlier pages was my role model. I wanted to do everything she did including going to college. Personally, college was beyond what I could have imagined, however because Lena was going that meant I had to go also. I felt if I made it through high school, then that would be good enough. Honestly, learning in an academic setting was never something I really enjoyed. I wanted to drop out at 16-years-old. Despite my crazy desires, I kept going to school.

During Lena's senior year of high school, we went to the Indiana Black Expo in downtown Indianapolis. As we explored all the exhibits hot, sweaty and thirsty, I could not help but notice her gathering college applications and putting them in her bag. So, I got some and put them in my bag too. In my heart, I had absolutely no intentions on really completing and mailing them in, however I refused to be left out.

I filled out every application. To my amazement, I got accepted to Indiana State, Ball State, Anderson University and Wilberforce Universities. Lena is nine months older than me; therefore, she had graduated high school and started at Ball State in Muncie, Indiana a year before me. Needless to say, in deciding where to send my fifty dollars deposit, hands down it would be Ball State University. After all, I knew people in Muncie and Lena was there, so off to Ball State I went.

The day my father was moving me and all my purple plastic totes to Muncie, Indiana, I had a surreal moment. Everything felt real, yet unreal all at the same time. I can remember weeping, feeling distressed and scared. But I knew that once I got in my grandpa's van, my daddy was not going to turn around no matter how much I screamed, hollered, or said that I made a mistake. My daddy was not going to waste his gas on me changing my mind. Bringing me back home on the same day was absolutely out of the question.

When he was moving my things into the dorm, I stood outside in the steamy heat staring up at the clouds. I was trippin'. I stood in complete disbelief that I was actually on a collage campus and not just to visit.

I saw a multitude of nationalities. There were people from various ethnic backgrounds with different skin colors, and some even spoke languages that I had never heard. I had a major culture shock.

After my dad moved in all my things he said to me, "Genie, welcome to the 'Halls of Higher Education', many will enter and few will finish. Call me if you want to come home in a few weeks and I will come get you."

The first couple of days on campus, I found myself crying on and off as I went through the process of getting adjusted to my new home. In this new world, I was forced to grow up fast. I had to make decisions like choosing a major, how to spend my money, how to use my time, and selecting a church to attend. Each choice was crucial and making the wrong decision could cost me big time!

I found myself bored because I was spending a lot of time in my dorm room. I hated the boredom but I was afraid to explore the campus. My entire life was basically spent around all African American people like me. And honestly I was highly intimated by other ethnic groups. When my cousin Mya, who lives in Muncie called me to see if I was okay; I told her I wanted to go home. The cultural diversity was too much for me. I felt defeated before I got started. I had always been taught that people of European decent were smarter and that they did not want to see people like me get ahead. It is amazing the lies we can embrace as the gospel truth.

In lieu of my very pessimistic attitude Mya said, I was going to go to church with her. That was a really great suggestion. My other cousin was also a member of the church and I remembered the pastors' wife from TM youth camp. So, I was excited about going. I welcomed leaving the dorms and seeing another face that looked like mine.

Upon going into the church I was very astonished. The church was multicultural as well. The church was also filled with young people, which made it very lively. People were singing songs that I did not know, but they sounded really good. While the "Praise and Worship" was going forth, God used a lady singing in the choir to talk about everything that I had been just feeling. I was shocked and touched beyond words. I started to cry. My mind was filled with all my years of going to church moreover I had never seen or heard anything remotely resembling what I was experiencing in that moment. The same choir member was speaking in tongues; that didn't surprise me; however what was being interrupted stunned me. Everything that I had been experiencing was being acknowledged. I knew that was God because that lady did not know me at all. From that moment on, I have enjoyed my spiritual journey of growing and learning at Christ Temple Global Ministries.

Back at school when classes actually got started I was not prepared for the giants I had to face. I remember sitting in the front of my English 101 course and all the students were chatting about the books they read in high school and over the summer and how they wrote term papers.

I had never written a real research paper and I only read one book in high school. That was *A Tale of Two Cities*. The Gary Community School did not prepare me for college in any way. I was behind academically. So needless to say, I got an F on the first paper. I messed up in a horrific way. The teacher was aware of the students that came from Gary Schools and because she knew that it was not intentional she allowed me another chance to write the paper. With one-on-one help, I did much better the second time.

College courses were a mental shock at first. I just knew I was going to be expelled because I was not smart enough. However, with God's divine assistance, I ultimately ended up doing all right.

In English, after a few more sessions at the writing center and help from others, I felt more confident. Then, it was on to Math

125. I knew I was doomed for sure this time. I did not understand anything that was taught the entire semester. It felt like the professor was speaking a language that I had never heard and she refused to translate what she was saying to help me understand. It was so bad I would just leave the class crying. Even, when I asked for help, I still did not comprehend the concepts. I felt really dumb, and to make matters worse, I was the only African-American in the class. In my mind, I felt like the other students were able to grasp the information because they were better prepared in high school. One day, Mya came to class with me so she could try to help me to do my homework. I still messed up; I just could not comprehend anything in that class. God truly gave me a miracle on that final exam. I got a C on the test so I got a D in the class. I am not promoting low grades but that truly was the best I could do. After you have done your very best, that is all you can do. I had to learn that lesson real quick.

In high school, I took general math for two years and then pre-algebra and algebra. It was by God's grace that I passed those classes. I can do the basics adding, subtracting, multiplying, division and money management. So, imagine how lost I was in a college math class with all those different terms and equations.

When considering a major, I knew that I wanted to help children and families in some way. I thought I would make a great teacher, but that required too many math classes. So I took a Social Work class the first semester. I enjoyed what I was learning and could personally relate to the study material, so I declared Social Work as my major. For so long, I felt like the child welfare system failed me, so I wanted to learn how I could make a positive difference in that crazy, flawed governmental program.

During my freshmen year of college, I longed to go back to the familiar sights and sounds of Gary, Indiana. However, I knew that there were some lessons that I needed to learn in Muncie, Indiana.

The pastor's wife called, "The First Lady" of the ministry invited me over to her family's home for dinner a few Sundays into the semester. Her approach was so kind and genuine that I could not resist. As I sat at the end of Sunday morning worship service talking about wanting to go back to Gary, the first lady walked up to me and began to speak in a very nurturing, calm, mother-like voice as she gently rubbed my lower ear. She asked me not to leave yet, but to come to her house for dinner for a couple of weeks. Going to the Millben's home was refreshing and fun. We sat at the table and ate good food and got to know each other. The Millben family became a safe haven for me. Just coming to church and having a place to really feel connected made me want to stay. There were some Sundays when Lena and I would walk over to their home to just relax and get away from the dorms.

In September, Christ Temple Global Ministries always had a Women's Retreat. After only being in Muncie a few weeks I was asked if I wanted to go. I was really skeptical. I had never attended a Women's Retreat before, but because the first lady asked me to go, I went.

Upon arriving I thought it would be women sitting around sharing sob stories and doing a lot of crying. I did not want to hear anything that would remind me of what I wanted so desperately to put behind me. Well, I was completely wrong. There was a lady there who wrote a book about her life, she also shared her testimony. As I sat there, I thought it was really powerful but I was not going to cry or let any of that power get to me. I had made up my mind not to let my guard down and not to show any feelings even if I was blessed by something or someone. Well by the Saturday afternoon session I was real soft, I felt my guard slippin'. Another lady got up and was just sharing the goodness of God. I do not recall it being anything that resembled a traumatic story, but the power of God began to move on me and I started to cry uncontrollably. One of the ladies came over and started to pray with me. She asked me if I wanted to talk and I said, "I don't know." Then she asked me, if I wanted to talk to Pastor Millben and I said "yes".

When I got to Pastor Millben I was still crying, but I had gained some level of composure. She was sitting on this swinging bench outside in a semi sunny spot with sunglasses on. She invited me to sit down, again with that same gentle voice. As I began to share, I was reassured that it was safe to talk. So, I shared as much as I could about what I was feeling regarding my life. Then the lady who wrote the book came over and sat by me on the swing and prayed with me. It was during this retreat that I became completely convinced that there was more God wanted to do with me and show me in Muncie, Indiana.

God prevailed and my grades came out okay. I was blessed to complete my freshmen year of college. During the summer, I went back to stay with my aunt and her family in another city and worked a summer job. I can remember feeling very special when I got a letter in the mail from Pastor Millben. Then, she came to have lunch with me at Applebee's. During our lunch, I became convinced that Pastor Millben was more than just my pastor; she had become the mother I had spent many years searching for. God ordained the way we connected. I never thought that I would be able to experience having a mother figure to love me despite all the mistakes I made in the past and would make in the future. But God did it. From that summer on, Pastor Millben became "Mom" to me!

In the fall as I returned to Ball State as a sophomore, I had some trials but for the most part, it was a good year. That was also the year I learned to drive.

As Christians, my friend and I decided not to date, but rather focus on our studies and growing in God. As a result, Valentine's Day was a hard day to enjoy being single. We both saw other young ladies in our dorm receiving flowers and balloons. They were getting all dressed up going out to dinner and everyone just looked happy. My roommate and I rested on our twin sized wooden framed beds and just talked about how we wished we could have gotten a token of love on Valentine's Day. My roommate said she would have been blissful if she could just get a dandelion. I said I would be delighted if I could just get one of those white pollen flowers that grow with the dandelions that you can just blow. After spending some time talking, we both decided that we did not want to have a man just for the sake of the holiday. We both knew and understood that could be a bad idea. So we coined the phrase "No More Dandelions." This statement means that we wouldn't just settle for a man, but we would wait for the mate God has for us. To be real honest, I did not want to be in a relationship; I just wanted all the cool stuff I saw other girls receiving.

I started to really grow in God in my new church environment. However, when my mom and I did talk it always ended up in an argument. I hated to argue, so our conversations were very few! I also hated that, but that was the only way I could survive having her in my life.

During the second semester of my sophomore year, I received some of the most shocking and disturbing news of my life. After an appointment at the local health center for a routine check-up, I found out that something was possibly wrong with me, for which there was no cure. The nurse practitioner informed me that she saw some abnormal white cells in my blood test. She also stated that it looked like I had Herpes, which could prevent me from having children.

I can't explain all of the emotions that I felt. I experienced a combination of anger, shame, being upset and bewilderment. I wanted so desperately for this to be a nightmare that I would wake up from. As that hot fall day progressed, it became more real that this was not a bad dream, but a reality that I had to face.

I thank God that I had the support of some of my trusted church family members as I waited for the test results to come back.

I can remember standing in 6:00 a.m. prayer on the following Sunday hearing Mom praying for me. When I first got the news, I walked to the church feeling so angry and frustrated that

I could have killed someone with my looks. As I sat and talked to the secretary, I poured out my heart about this crisis. She just sat and listened. This was another point in my life when I felt completely vulnerable and questioned why and how this could happen to me. I was not sexually active at all. However, just talking it out helped me to gain some much needed self-control as my fury turned into disappointment.

I was quickly reminded of the healing and miracle power that is in God. It took several days, but I pulled myself together. After a couple of days, I got a call from the doctor's office and they said it was not Herpes but that I needed more test done. That put my mind and heart at ease. I decided not to go back to the doctor. Instead, I chose to trust in God!

In July of 2002, I graduated from Ball State University. That was one of the best days of my life.

God has blessed my life beyond all that I could have imagined! So the theme of my under graduate college career was trials, training, trusting, transitions, and triumphs!

CHAPTER EIGHT

In the Hallway: Between the Promise and the Prize

In your patience possess ye your souls.

Luke 21:19, KJV

I had done it! I had endured four years of college; I was armed with my degree and ready to conquer the world, or so I thought.

I thought the simple fact that I completed a bachelor's degree would guarantee me a good paying job with benefits. To my dismay, there was no real emphasis on the employment outlook after graduation in any of my courses. We were just told Social Workers are always in high demand. I only knew that graduating was a great milestone that I had accomplished.

As was my case, I had no solid workable plan for obtaining a job that was in my field. Instantly, I learned if you fail to plan, you plan to fail! With no real concrete plan in place after graduation, I found myself working at a daycare to pay my bills and to keep my mind semi-occupied so I would not completely surrender to feeling like a total failure.

After working long hours, I would still walk home to my apartment and look for employment in what I had spent four years training for. Due to my lack of career planning, employment networking and focusing all my attention on the excitement of the moment, everything that led up to graduation day was focused on the party and all my family and friends coming to celebrate this miraculous milestone in my life. I did not have any new goals or any idea of what I could do to start the journey of life after college.

When people asked me what I was going to do, I really did not know. I just said move and work. Yeah, right!!!! I did not have a plan or money to support any kind of move or plan for that matter. I just said what I thought people wanted to hear. After all, how could I go to school for four years and still be clueless? But in reality, I had no clue what I wanted to do. All I knew was that I enjoyed working with children and families. I knew I was good at doing that!

Each time I applied for a job and went on an interview I got a "sorry you are not the person we are looking for" letter. Those letters really stink when you are in the hallway of life waiting for some positive changes to occur.

After a few rejection letters and no idea of what to do next, I continued to work at the local daycare. My confidence in my skills along with self-worth became very low. I felt like I was not good at anything but caring for babies and children. Caring for children and babies is a gift from God, but I knew that I had other talents as well. My mind could not see anything outside of Elgin Street; the street on which I lived and worked.

During my Elgin Street experience, many things in my life changed. One day, on a job hunting quest, my cousin who was my roommate, her Goddaughter, and myself were driving up to northwestern Indiana and then on to the Illinois area for a job interview. That day, I was feeling hopeful and felt like things were going to start to look up for me if I got this job. I could finally switch my mental label from failure to success because I would be working in my field and making more money.

On December 5, 2002, while in route on this cloudy day, we were involved in a very serious car accident on I-65 North. There were snow flurries blowing in the air along with some patches of black ice on the highway. We were traveling in the left hand lane listening to Lamar Campbell, *"I Want to be Closer to You"* while our speed was approximately 65mph.

All of a sudden, our Maroon 2002 Pontiac Grand Pre rolled over five times. We landed wheels up in the air in the median. The windows shattered instantly but my cousin was able to get out the car and she was able to pull her Goddaughter out.

However, I was not able to get out, I was trapped! I could not move at all. I cannot express to you how terrified I was. I knew if I died in that moment all my church going and outreach efforts in high school would have been in vain. I was going to go to Hell. No questions about it. I knew my heart was not right and I had not even begun to explore the depth of the calling God placed on my life. While I was stuck in the car upside down feeling the heat of something pressing against my body, I felt like the Lord was warning me to get right and get busy with the things He had placed in my heart to do.

As the rescue workers were attempting to cut me out the car, I began to tell them that God had a plan for their lives. The rescue workers kept asking me what day it was, to make sure that I was alert. As they asked me the day of the week I kept telling them God had a plan for them. When they finally cut me out the car, my right shoulder was broken, and the pain was mind-boggling. While they placed my cold, weak body on that cold stretcher, they began cutting all my clothes off. The only thing I remember was seeing the feathers from my new coat flying in the air. I was in tremendous pain, but I was more concerned about not having a coat. You see, I had just bought that one a few weeks earlier. I asked the workers what they were doing. They just keep assuring me that I was going to be okay. As I lay on the stretcher all I could think was why? why? why? Me and another bright idea!!

Was this entirely my fault, because I was trying to find a job again?

Upon arriving at the hospital, I remember being in the cold, white emergency room, surrounded by all sorts of medical devices. I was covered with warm blankets and reminded that my cousin and her Goddaughter were doing well. I was told by the emergency doctors and nurses not to move at all. That was not a problem; I was in too much pain to even consider moving an inch.

Shortly after being alone with my thoughts, the police came to get a report about what happened. Then my other cousin, aunt, and uncle came in. I was grateful to be alive to see them. My aunt made me feel better. I told her of my pain levels and she stated, "Girl, I thought you were dead, thank God you are alive to feel the pain!"

For the rest of my hospital short stay, I had to rely completely on the help of the nurses and my family. It was a very real humbling experience. The acts of kindness really touched my heart.

After my cousin, her Goddaughter and I were all released from the hospital, our family and friends came straight to my grandmother's house to check on us. Each person did anything they could to help. When I saw my best friend walk in the door I knew everything was going to be fine. Just her presence gave me hope!

Grateful to be alive, the next day we got ourselves together and my cousins went to gather our clothes and to look for my eye glasses amidst all the shattered glass and debris. That night, my cousin preached at my uncle's church. She went and really ministered from the heart of God. My best friend gave me a coat out of her car to wear to the church service. She patiently helped me with everything and bought food for me to eat and to share with my family. That was a true blessing from God. I have made special mention of all of the acts of kindness, because I understand that people don't have to be nice to you. And again it is a true blessing when you have family and friends that love you from the heart!

Upon arriving back in Muncie, I was ordered to be off of work for about ten weeks. For the first few weeks, all I could do was sleep, take pain pills, and go to the doctor. However, I did go to church, grateful that God had spared our lives. I gave God all the glory and praise. I knew at that point, I needed to really get focused on the things God wanted me to do and to make some spiritual changes.

From a child, I knew the Lord had a special calling on my life, despite all the hell I suffered physically, mentally and emotionally.

One night in my sleep I heard the Lord speak to me and say, "I called you!"

Although I did not want to receive it, God was calling me to speak His Word. To share the Gospel with who were lost and had real issues. In reality, I knew it! However, I felt like I was not good enough. I was not what I could, should, or wanted be in God. I can recall that even as a child, I used to have many dreams. In some of the dreams, I was preaching. I would have on a long white robe and I would feel the presence of God as I was speaking. The more I spoke the stronger the power of God became in each dream.

In one of the dreams, I was preaching at the church I grew up in. That was the place where many of my battles were fought. These dreams scared me so bad that I would wake up saying "no" out loud. "God can't use me to help anyone because I am not serving Him to the best of my ability." I also felt that I didn't know how to as child and a young teenager.

During my time of healing I did a lot of soul searching. I asked God why He allowed me to live through that horrific car accident. Again, God reminded me of my childhood dreams and many other prophetic words that had been spoken over me. I knew I had to get serious, but I did not know what to do. I read my Bible, prayed, and watched Christian T.V.

After a while, I found myself bored and searching for what to do next. I had given up on looking for a new job because that hadn't proved to be productive at all. But, I was still searching for something.

After ten weeks, I went back to work feeling really bad about my lack of what I called *success*. I became depressed. I was tired of walking to work in the cold and snow. Feeling closed in by Elgin Street and wishing I had a way out, I came up with an idea. I was going back to school! The institution that I disliked became the system that I had learned how to function in. School had structure and set rules. That seemed to be the system that I could be *successful* in.

I began to search for colleges that I did not have to take the Graduate Record Examination to get into. I was blessed to find Case Western Reserve University in Cleveland, Ohio. I applied and was accepted. My father and his God-sister took me to Cleveland to check out the campus and to look for an apartment. I was again hopeful that this was going to be my big break and I would become *successful* at something else besides caring for children. I got there and all appeared to look good. I applied for an apartment and got rejected due to things being on my credit report. By this time, I had accumulated medical bills from the automobile accident. I returned to Muncie, feeling defeated but relieved at the same time. I wanted to move, but in my heart I felt like I would fail at being a graduate student. So, I was back at the faithful daycare working very hard. Not knowing what else to do, and to relieve my frustration, I turned to writing.

Eugenia Rollins

Elgin Street
Up and down,
Hot and Cold,
Rain and Snow,
This street has inhabited my life.
Work and Home,
Home and Work,
Elgin Street has been a testing ground for my soul.
Working' every day to pay the bills, but the bills still ain't getting paid.
Is the world bigger than Elgin Street?
I feel like I am trapped in a maze of highs and lows on this street called Elgin.
11/7/02

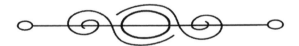

Back at work, my boss had become very callous and began to speak very condescending to me. My work performance was good and to my understanding, no complaints had been registered against me. In a meeting, she stated that the only reason she allowed me to continue working was because she did not want me to be without a paycheck. My boss felt I should be employed in my area of study. I agreed with her but what was I to do when all my efforts were failing? Knowing that my time was swiftly coming to an end, I just started passing out my resume to anyone who I thought might know someone. This time, I was blessed to give my resume to one of the counselors who came in to see some of the children. I got an interview for a case manager position and then I got the job. My world was bright again.

My new job would give me an increase in pay and I got to learn more about the field of social work. I had a desk, business cards, my own phone line and most of all, I would get to help families at a greater capacity. This was a true step up.

I started this job on May 4, 2004. I was very excited about being a case manager. I welcomed the challenge of helping families and children. After all, this is what I was good at. For the first couple of months, I woke up excited about work. I packed lunch and went to work each day like it was an adventure. I was completing case notes, attending staff meetings, and working with families. It couldn't get better!

After about six months on the job, my excitement died out. I think it might have started after I went into a client's home and a man there made a direct sexual advance at me. This man was very tall, un-groomed and very frightening. The house had very little lighting and there were roaches crawling everywhere. Literally!! I was so scared and did not know what to do. I was afraid to leave but I did not want to stay. That job became a real learning ground from that point on. I loved working with the kids, but some of the cases I saw reminded me of some personal things that I had encountered.

During some of the team meetings, I would hear some of my team members speak very unsympathetically about some of the cases. One time in particular, a team member was making jokes about a client's level of intelligence. That hurt me as if they had talked about me personally. All I could think about was what if it was my family or friends under their case load? The verbal cruelty was too much for me to bear while carrying my secret sores from the past. As the agency was undergoing some management changes, I was afforded the opportunity to resign as a result of not signing a Non-Compete Document. I honestly, did not agree with the terms of the contract, so I did not sign. That decision might have been immature on my part, but I decided that for the rest of my life I did not want to work for that agency anymore! One year later, I was done with that case management job.

I was in my own process of healing. Although I chose to leave, being at that agency gave me greater experiences to apply to my resume. But greater than adding to my career, the agency added to my life. For one, I found that I was able to do more than care for children in a daycare setting. That was major. I was also blessed to work with a teen group and specifically a teen girls group. I was a blessing to them but they were more of a blessing to me. Having them come in and benefit from my classroom skills and my wisdom actually helped enhanced me as a person and a professional.

Some days I would go home feeling like I really did make a difference in the lives of my clients. That job was also an asset to me in that I learned how to maintain professional relationships with my co-workers. Overall, when I think about it, working for the agency was like the *Tale of Two Cities*. It was the best and the worst of times.

For two or three months after the job was over I found myself driving pass there to see who was there. I was very disheartened at how things ended and again started to second guess my decision. I began to wish that things had ended differently. One day in particular as I was driving pass again, The Holy Spirit came to me and said, "Do not look back! Look at how much better you feel after leaving that job."

I began to notice that my hair, which had been falling out from stress, was growing again. I also felt better when I would wake up in the mornings. The job had been good and had added more experiences to my resume, also allowing me to get my own apartment, and a car to get around in. I was no longer on Elgin Street. Thank You Jesus!!! And last but not least, I was not feeling afraid of my life being threatened by going into the homes of strangers. There was no longer a feeling of dread from the thought of having to go to work. I was free!

With the sunshine, comes the rain. Well, the rainy part of my situation was, I was jobless. I was now looking for a job all over again. But, this time I had an apartment and a car to pay for, with no job in sight.

For some reason, I felt confident that I would find a new job quickly. So, after filing for my unemployment benefits, I took my time looking for the right offer. I felt like I was on the road to a blessing. It was like catching a glimpse of the victory ahead, like standing in the hallway of life waiting to walk in the door to receive a great prize.

An example of receiving one of many prizes was during the time that I was still on unemployment, one my biggest dreams came true. One Sunday while I was in Sunday school, we were asked to talk about one of our biggest hopes. My biggest hope was to go Disney World. I had always dreamed about what it would be like to see "Mickey Mouse." There was a family at the church who heard me say this. The family invited me dinner that Sunday. During dinner the family asked me to go with them on their family vacation to Disney World. I was completely stunned; I thought there had to be a catch to such a wonderful offer. This was too good to be true.

I had to ponder this for a couple days, but then I decided to go. I had the best time. We drove a really nice camper to Florida. When we arrived at Disney World, it was at night and we approached the red sign that said "Walt Disney World", I started crying. I could not believe that my dream had come true.

As the week unfolded, I saw many Disney characters and I got to have lunch with Winnie the Pooh. That just blew my 25 year old mind. I smiled so much that week, and it really felt like a good dream that I never wanted to end. I did not know it then, but this family would become a very special part of my life. It is and has been because of their gentle Godly approach that I have made some of the good choices in my life. Disney World was the beginning of a wonderful relationship. I am forever grateful for each and every person that God has ever sent in my life to point me in the right direction. So, as I continued to wait in the hallway of life, God sent me reminders to assure me that he had not forgotten his promises to me.

During this season, I enrolled in Christian Counseling to deal with the issues that continued to silently haunt me night and day. This was my second attempt at counseling. Although I was not confident it would help, I still knew that I had to make an attempt at it. For the first couple of weeks, I just sat and the counselor did most of the talking. I was careful not to say too much for fear that she would change her view of me or that I would begin to open up and then she would stop talking to me. To the Glory of God, this time was different.

At first I did not talk much but I looked forward to going every week. Eventually, I began to share and allowed myself to feel a variety of emotions. I felt things that I had not felt in years. Things that I had buried to survive came alive again; anger, disappointment, hurt, and many other emotions. The only difference was that I had a safe place to honestly talk about how I felt without being judged. There were times when I would just come in, talk, and then we would pray and all I could do was cry. The tears felt like they were cleansing and healing my soul.

Some of the stories I shared with my counselor, I was afraid no one would believe, but she did. She was such a blessing in my life. There were times during my counseling process that I wanted to stop because of the pain from my past. Choosing to make choices was empowering but very difficult. However, I dared not stop, I wanted to be healed and healed for good!

For a long time, I had let everyone else make my choices, and the ones that I did make; they were based on wanting to be loved and accepted by others. A person can never be true to themselves while always trying to please others.

One of my biggest anxieties was to allow myself to really open up to friends. Part of my healing was confronting certain friends. If I had made a different choice than they had, I needed to be honest, and not be afraid of their rejection.

There were homework assignments to complete each week. There were days when I could not bring myself to actually complete some of the assignments. I would do as many as I could then I would stop.

One assignment that comes to mind that I was instructed to complete was to keep a journal daily. This journal was to consist of my thoughts and feelings and I was to note anytime I felt anger. In this journal, I was also instructed to keep a food log. Eating on a consistent basis has been a struggle for me for many years. Writing down my food allowed me to see that I needed some serious help and that with God this can be conquered. I am better, but this is an area that I am yet allowing God to work on with me. In my journal, I would scribble so hard that I would tear holes in the paper. As time progressed the scribbling got to be less and I was able to put my feelings into words. Things that were troubling me to the core were getting better with much prayer.

One of the major differences that I saw in myself was that I was able to talk to my mother without having a major blow up each time. I was able to know when I had enough and end the conversation. My family even noticed that at family gatherings, we did not argue as usual. As I have learned, healing is a continual journey. I am continuing to work on being open and honest with her. I am learning what to say and what not to say, and how to say it and to say sorry when I am wrong. I can truly say that God is really blessing my efforts. Within the last year, I told my mother and father of the sexual abuse that happened when I was growing up. That is really a miracle from God.

With no options left, after much prayer and working with my counselor and another friend, I decided to apply to graduate school again. Due to lack of finances I contacted Case Western Reserve University to see if my application was still good. I was informed that it was not, but that it would not cost me anything to reapply. I did reapply and I got accepted for the second time.

As God would have it, I moved to Cleveland, Ohio and attended Case Western Reserve University. I worked very hard and earned a Master's Degree in Social Work and now I am a Licensed Social Worker. God had brought me a long way from that little girl in Gary, IN, who some said could never learn or be anything worthwhile.

What I will tell you is this: all of us will experience the "Hallways" of life. There is never much in a hallway; it's just designed to take you from one place to the next. But rest assured that the "Promises" God makes to you in the hallway will ultimately led to the "Prizes" on the other side of the door!

CHAPTER NINE

A Lesson Learned Is A Lesson Never to Repeat

I will not die; instead, I will live to tell what the Lord has done. (NLT)

Psalms 118:17

I was left to die on the church pew but God had a bigger and better plan for my life. I proclaim to you that I am still standing. Against all the odds, I made it. There are many things that I have learned along the way, some of which I will share to the Glory of God.

I have learned that there will always be a test to work something in or out of you. Only God knows the appointed time for test to begin and end. God will either grant you the grace and strength to go through the test or he will bring it to an end. Complaining will not make the test end faster. Success and freedom may look different for each and every individual. My freedom has come by accomplishing the goal of placing the testimony God has given me in this book. Being a voice for the voiceless, through my testimony, has set me free.

Some test you will understand and others you won't. However, true faith trusts God even when you cannot see your way. With time, prayer, and spiritual guidance, God has taught me to trust Him when I am completely helpless in making sense of life. Each trial has made me a stronger person. Though I could not see it at the time, the anguish I went through has put me in a position to effectively empower men, women, boys, and girls to see beyond their present tribulations and to see that there is hope through a real relationship with Jesus Christ.

I have also learned that if at first you do not succeed, do not give up. Take some time to gather your thoughts, and emotions through prayer and honest self-examination, get a realistic, workable plan and then try again. Attempt to do something different so that you will get a positive result. The example that comes to my mind is when I was learning to drive. I found driving to be very hard at first. I would get sad when my instructors would say "you really need to work on turning and driving in your own lane." I thought I would never get a driver's license. Each time I wanted to quit, but with sadness, frustration, and determination I kept going back until I got better. Consequently, after many trials, I finally got my driver's license. I have learned to drive and stay in my own lane in life. I can only do what God has empowered me to accomplish.

When the stresses of life come to get us down, we have to lean on God and gather a true support network. Get prayer, get focused, and give it the very best that you have. Press through the tears, confusion, and any other thought or feeling that may come to oppose or abort your dream. Dreams can become a reality.

Eugenia Rollins

Life also taught me that there will be people who will come and go in your life, but God will send some people to remain in your life forever. The key is to know who is supposed to stay, and who will only remain for a season.

While some relationships are only for a season, it is essential that you glean and/or deposit what you are supposed to, so that time will not be wasted. God only knows who He has ordained to be life-long friends. Do not force a friendship if it is not meant to be. You will bring more undue stress and heartache than what is needed. In addition, people's roles may change in your life, though it may feel uncomfortable, it is very necessary at times. Some of my beloved mentor's as a teen have become my valued friends and prayer partners as an adult. I once looked to them for guidance and support now they come to me when they need help. I have to admit this has been a difficult lesson for me, but as I have gotten older I understand a little more each day.

I found that letting go can be very difficult to do. I had a friend that I thought would remain in my life forever. However, she decided that she did not want to be my friend anymore. This reminded me of the rejection that I lived with as a child. I did not

118

handle this situation in the ideal way. Her decision left me confused and upset.

Nevertheless, God prevailed and helped me to see the bigger picture. It was me; I had a problem with letting go. Take what you learned from each person and situation and move on. Always be grateful for the good times you have shared with God's people and know that new people will come into your life as God sees fit.

The waiting process can be long and isolating, but it is in these times that God wants us to come closer to Him, so He can do with us what He ordained. I can now see how the waiting process has strengthened my life. It has given me time to deal with me, and to align myself closer to God without distractions.

It is important not to compare our life process with others. Everything and everyone in life grows and matures at different paces. My process may have taken longer because there are lessons that I have had to glean to be a stronger person in order to help the people God will place in my path. Sometimes, it becomes easy to see what we think is success in other people's lives and think "what is wrong with me? Why aren't I where they appear to be? Why are things in my life always a test?" Perhaps, God is attempting make you stronger than your test. The test may not always move but God will give you strength to go through it and come out with victory.

I have found that in order to get better, you have to see yourself as better. Transition is not an event, but a consistent process. You have to be really committed to change because it will not come without a battle.

In order to change my life for the good, I had to see myself doing some things differently. For one, I had to see that I could do good things. It was very tough for me to recognize that I could achieve high-quality goals with just God's help. I had been taught to depend on people for everything in my life, not even really thinking my own thoughts. I depended on people to the extent that I could not make any choices by myself without fear that I was making a bad choice. God continues to assist me in seeing that I can make fine decisions.

Being in Cleveland, Ohio is a decision that I made with prayer. This was a very great step for me. God gave me what I needed each step of the way. Upon arrival I was very worried and on my own. I knew that God wanted me to move and I do not regret the choice. It has not been easy but it was definitely worth it. You should not always look for people to support the vision God gives to you. Think about it, that is why it is the vision that He gave to YOU! God will send provision and people to support your vision but do not expect everyone to see where God is taking you.

I have learned to never judge a person by the way they come across. The way we perceive is our reality. Sometimes our realities of others are false. When different church members would say to me, "be nice, smile, it ain't that bad," they did not know the depth of the mental distress I was enduring. Most people can and will respond to consistent, pure love and care. Even people that we feel are very rude and mean. Typically there are reasons why a person conducts themselves in certain ways. Sometimes they are aware of their behavior and other times they are not. This lesson can be especially difficult when working through your own issues. God can and will help you to love all people and put them in the correct place in your life if you ask Him to help you with a serious heart alteration. This has been a continual process for me. I expect that this is a lesson that will be life-long.

You can never go wrong as long as you let Jesus be the Lord of your life. You may say well, I have never heard Jesus speak to me, and how can I let someone I cannot see with my natural eyes lead me? Well, first you have to believe that Jesus is real and that He cares about everything in your life. Then you have to know that He has a plan for your life and every experience you have been through, are going through, and will go through.

It is not God's will for any man to perish (to die), but for everyone to come to repentance. It is essential to acknowledge the fact that you are a sinner. A sinner is a person that has committed an action or thought that is against God. We are all born sinners. The Bible states in Romans 3:23, *"For all hath sinned and come short of the glory of God."(KJV)* That is not by any fault of your own, in the Holy Bible according to Romans 10:9-10, it states that *"if thou shalt confess with thy mouth the Lord Jesus, and shalt believe in thine heart that God hath raised Him from the dead, thou shalt be saved."* In verse 10 it states: *"For with the heart man believeth unto righteousness: and with the mouth confession is made unto salvation. (KJV)*

After all of my suffering, and enduring the process of healing, I now realize that God placed me here on the earth to be a blessing to people. Being transparent is one of the ways God wants to use me to assist people. So, if God can use the testimony He gave me to help someone else then it has been worth it all!

In conclusion, it is my prayer that your faith has been renewed, your heart strengthened, and that you feel empowered to step up in some way to make a positive difference in the life of a child or teen in your church or community. If everyone could reach someone, then we could make a big difference in the world. Just as God was with me on my journey, so He is with you. Whether you are a child, teen, or adult, He will give you what you need to live a life of victory and peace.

Jeremiah 33:3 (KJV) says, *"Call unto me and I will answer thee and show thee great and mighty things with thou knowest not."* Sincerely call on God today and be honest about what you desire and according to His will, He will show up! Salvation is ours, by the mighty power of God!

Thank you for the opportunity to share my testimony with you. I pray that your life has been enriched in some fashion. Until my next book may, God Bless you.

Eugenia Rollins

To contact the author for questions, comments, or public speaking events please e-mail: missrollinsii@yahoo.com.

64043098R00070

Made in the USA
Lexington, KY
26 May 2017